Cultivating Awa
A Prac

ENCOUNTER
JESUS

SARAH CROCKETT

Encounter Jesus: Cultivating Awareness and Intimacy – A Practical Guide
Copyright © 2018 Sarah Crockett, beENCOUNTERed, LLC.
www.beENCOUNTERed.com

Cover Design: Sarah Crockett
Formatting: Sarah Crockett & Amanda Shearon
Editors: Samuel Lloyd, Mary G. Crockett, Kaitlin Macleer, Caroline Anderson,
Jonathan Bugden, and Chelsea White

ISBN-13: 978-1986479769

Unless otherwise indicated, all Scripture quotations are taken from the New
International Version.

Note: The author uses special capitalization when referring to Father God, Jesus, & Holy Spirit.

DEDICATION

More than a book, Encounter Jesus has been a process of discovery, growth, and healing. I dedicate this book to all the people who have encouraged and helped along the way. Thank you Jason White, Chelsea White, Katie Macleer, Rachel McPherson, Ron Vunkannon, Les Hardin, Karen Hardin, Heather White, Samuel Lloyd, Amanda Shearon, and Mary Crockett. A special thank you to Sandi Krakowski, Jeremy Krakowski, Caroline Anderson, and Jonathan Bugden for sharing their wisdom and experience. We did it!

TABLE OF CONTENTS

FORWARD

It is my pleasure and with much excitement I would like to introduce you to the book Encounter Jesus, a book that will take you on an adventure with Jesus. I believe it is a 'NOW' read which brings the living reality of intimacy that so many long for and which Jesus desires with us. He says He never leaves us or forsakes us and there is a living reality about that. He is not a God that is afar off, He is a God who is real, loves to chat and talk to us. He participates in what we are doing whether it is writing emails, cooking a meal, driving a car, talking to the someone in grocery store, or a meeting at work - He is there all the time. Encounter Jesus will bring you into encounters of an extra-ordinary kind with Him, and experience the reality of the scriptures 'Christ in me the hope of glory' (Colossians 1:27) and, 'your real life is hidden with Christ in God' (Colossians3:3).

Be prepared to have your life transformed as you encounter Jesus in this book. Keep a journal as you read it, take time with the activations, and I believe you will encounter Jesus in a new way. Sarah's testimonies and encounter activations will help you create a more intimate friendship with Jesus and come into the place of deep communing which will bring fulfillment like never before and usher you into the relationship God intended you to have with Him. I believe physical healing will take place as Jesus transcends your deepest emotions and joy will be released as in His presence. Encounter Jesus is written from Sarah's heart and it is an experience which can be yours too. Be prepared, you may never be the same again. Enjoy!

Caroline Anderson, CEO & Founder of CMA & Associates
Caroline has also been a director of Catch the Fire London and Co-Director, along with her late husband, of Restoring the Foundations UK and Europe.

INTRODUCTION

It is such an honor to have the opportunity to share this journey with you! I know from experience that just one moment in God's presence can change what I could never change in a lifetime. Just knowing that makes me super excited for all Jesus has planned. You've been set up! This is a divine appointment. Jesus has chosen this specific moment in your life to meet you and love in you specific ways, maybe like never before.

The first encounter with Jesus I ever remember having was at summer camp when I was fourteen. I started attending YMCA Camp Greenville in Cedar Mountain, North Carolina at the age of ten. Camp Greenville was my home away from home. The summer before I started going was the summer Camp Greenville became a co-ed camp and year after year there was a group of girls that were always in the same cabin with me. I loved camp and especially enjoyed getting away from the heat of the Florida summers and into the cool mornings and afternoon breeze of the Blue Ridge Mountains. I would spend the school year imagining and anticipating the adventures of the upcoming summer. Going to camp was the highlight of every summer, and this particular summer was my fifth summer going up to the mountain. It was my cabin's night to campout and it started raining so our counselors took us to Pretty Place, the camp's outdoor chapel on the side of the mountain overlooking the valley down below, for shelter. Sleeping on the concrete steps of the chapel didn't make for the most comfortable night of sleep and I woke up before anyone else. As I sat there wrapped up in my sleeping bag taking in the view and enjoying the brisk mountain air, I witnessed the most majestic sunrise I had ever seen in my entire life. Looking to my left, I could see the sun peeking over the top of the ridgeline. Purple, orange, and yellow hues began to paint the morning sky. There was a crispness in the air and sense of peace that surrounded me. As I took everything in, something inside of me deeply resonated with the beauty, awe, and wonder of that magnificent moment. Somehow, I just knew to invite whoever was behind this awesome display of beauty into my heart. In hindsight, I realized that I was encountering Jesus in that moment. Jesus is the Word (*John 1:1, 14*) and the Word of God is living and active (*Hebrews 4:12*), therefore, Jesus is living and active. I encountered the reality of Jesus that morning as the sun rose over the mountains. Years later as I grew in my knowledge and experience with scripture, I realized that I had received a revelation of *Romans 1:20* that day:

> *"Ever since the creation of the world His eternal power and divine nature, invisible though they are, have been understood and seen through the things He has made. So men are without excuse".*

This early morning encounter was the beginning of my journey in discovering who it was I had just encountered. I love how Jesus has this amazing way of taking Himself (the Word of God) and encountering us in specific and personal ways. I know He wants to do the same for you!

Prepare Your Heart to Encounter Jesus

Before reading any further, I want to encourage you to take a moment to posture your heart and open yourself to begin this journey with Jesus. Close your eyes and picture your heart. What does it look like? How does it feel? What does it need? What is it longing for?

Next, imagine Jesus standing in front of you. Look into His eyes as He stands before you. What do you see? How do you feel? Stay here for a moment and gaze into His eyes. Allow Jesus, the Lover of your soul, to gaze back into your eyes. As you stand there before one another let Jesus speak to you. This isn't a time to think or try to imagine what He is going to say. Just be…there…with Jesus. Listen with your eyes. Listen with your ears. Listen with your heart.

Finally, open your heart to go deeper in "trust[ing] in Him with all your heart and lean[ing] not on your own understanding" (*Proverbs 3:5-6*). Take a moment to remember that you have been given the "mind of Christ" (*1 Corinthians 2:16*) and He wants to do "immeasurably more than all you can ask or imagine" (*Ephesians 3:20*).

It's time. You're ready. This is your moment. Enjoy the journey and may this experience help you cultivate a lifestyle and a lifetime of encounters. I pray that you will be forever changed in the intimate presence of Jesus!

ENCOUNTER TESTIMONIES

CHAPTER 1
OBEYING THE NUDGE

Encounter Testimony

I was in grad school living just on the edge of campus. I had just been saved a year or two before this encounter and was learning and growing in my relationship with Jesus. I woke up in the middle of the night because I had to go to the bathroom. However, as I lay back down to fall asleep I had this strong sense that I should go to the Wesley prayer chapel. It was more of a knowing than a feeling, but I couldn't shake it. It was 2:30a.m. and the prayer chapel was on the opposite side of campus, but I just couldn't shake the nudge to go so I hopped in the car and headed that way.

I was waiting at a stop light at the corner of Dewey Street and Tennessee Street with a McDonalds on my left and campus just on the other side of the light. The next thing that happened I remember as if it were just yesterday. I heard His voice in my head say, "Pray with the girl that's there". My thoughts began to race. What if no one was there? What if there was a group of people? Yes, it was 2:3030a.m., but that's not unusual for college students. I was so tired I remember just choosing to believe Him.

I arrived at the prayer chapel about five minutes later and when I walked in I saw one girl sitting on the ground praying. I was in awe! I was honestly waiting for the heavens to open, angels to come down wrapped in glorious light and music to start playing. I had really, actually, specifically heard God's voice. I decided to introduce myself. We talked for awhile and seeing that it was getting even later I offered to pray for her. She agreed and again I was expecting the angels, light, and music to burst forth…nothing. By this time it was around 4a.m.. I offered her a ride home and dropped her off near my side of campus.

I drove away from her dorm that night excited that I had heard His voice, but with my heart questioning the purpose of it all. I chalked it up to learning to be obedient and shared the testimony when the opportunities arose. Two years after this encounter I was sitting in the mountains at Pretty Place spending time with Jesus when He reminded me of this encounter and finally shared the purpose of the encounter. I heard Him so clearly, "I needed you to take her home that night because something was going to happen to her when she walked home that night". I was speechless.

My Takeaways From This Encounter
- I don't need to know the purpose behind His requests to follow His voice
- I'm glad I don't always know what is attached to my obedience
- Jesus will go to great lengths to protect one of His sheep
- He sees, He knows, and He loves deeply
- Following His voice is a fun adventure

Reflection
What is Jesus speaking to you through this encounter testimony?

_____
_____
_____
_____
_____
_____
_____
_____

CHAPTER 2
GOOD REPORT

Encounter Testimony

I had been working as a College Life Coach for six months when my co-worker came into my office one morning to ask me to pray for her. What made this request interesting is that I had never had a conversation with this person beyond borrowing a phone charger twice. I agreed and asked her how I could pray for her specifically. She began to share how her washing machine was broken, along with her air conditioner not working. Her dog was also sick and the vet hadn't been able to figure out why. To top it all off, she and her husband had saved money for five years to go on their dream honeymoon and were leaving in a few days. She was overwhelmed, tired, and worried about leaving her fur-baby, but wasn't sure if they should cancel the trip.

I agreed to be in prayer for her and declared good reports over the washing machine, air conditioner, and dog. She thanked me and went back to her office. She was in and out of the office the next few days meeting repair men and trying to figure out if they would be able to go on their trip. Every time I would see her and get an update I would declare good reports over her. Two days before they were to fly out for their long-awaited honeymoon I got a text from her saying that the dog was getting worse. The text ended with her asking me what to do. I called her back, declared good reports, and led her through an encounter with Jesus. I had her imagine Jesus standing in front of her and told her that He was going to tell her something. He reassured her that everything was going to work out. Long story short, the washing machine got fixed, the air conditioner was repaired, the dog saw a specialist who was able to identify the problem, and they were able to fly out on time and enjoy their honeymoon!

My Takeaways From This Encounter
- Words have power, especially when I declare them in faith
- People can recognize Jesus in me without me having to say a word

- People need Jesus and Jesus needs me to know and release His presence wherever I go
- Small things, like loaning someone a phone charger, build bridges that lead to encounters

Reflection
What is Jesus speaking to you through this encounter testimony?

_____

_____

_____

_____

_____

_____

_____

_____

CHAPTER 3

JESUS REALLY LOVES ME

Encounter Testimony

It was a Thursday night and Valentine's Day was a few days away. The dread of spending, yet another, Valentine's Day alone was looming through my thoughts. Growing up dating wasn't much of a priority or on my radar at all. I was focused on academics and reaching my goal of being Valedictorian. Outside of academics I spent my afternoons and weekends playing and coaching soccer. When I got to college I dated a few guys here and there, but nothing ever developed into anything serious. Once again, my attention was focused on academics and extracurricular activities. It wasn't that I had no interest in dating I was just focused on other things. However, in hindsight, I realize that I didn't feel confident in myself, what I wanted, or how to move towards it. I was content in the ways I had chosen to spend my time and never really made dating a priority. So here I sat in my one-bedroom apartment in my mid-twenties feeling very aware of my singleness. I started sharing with Jesus how disheartening it was to live through another Valentine's Day and how lonely it felt. Even though I dated before, nothing had ever become serious and when I was dating it was never on February 14th. From my perspective, I had a lot of really good evidence for my argument - here I was in my late twenties and the prospect of marriage wasn't even a blip on the proverbial radar. I was living alone and surrounded by college students most of the time. My church was amazing, except for the fact that there was only one male within 10 years of my age in either direction. The impending Valentine's Day looked bleak. After a few minutes of venting, I heard Jesus whisper back to me, "I want to be your first Valentine". I responded in my thoughts, "Great, but I'd have to do everything and what kind of Valentine's Day is that?!" I left it at that and I went on about my evening.

The next day was a Friday, the day before Valentine's Day, I sat in our weekly staff meeting at the campus ministry where I worked at Florida State University. Our "office" was actually a room in a house on campus. Half way through the meeting, a woman from my church stopped in and asked for me. I got up from the meeting and met her at the door where she handed me a red lunch bag decorated with pink and purple hearts. She informed me that the Holy Spirit had prompted her to go to the store after church Wednesday night and had led her to buy some Valentine goodies for me. My jaw almost hit the floor! The conversation with Jesus the night before began to play in my head. I went back to my apartment in shock! It was one of those moments when something you know in your head becomes something you know in your heart. In that moment I knew Jesus loved me, but in this moment I knew He loved me specifically. I'd read all about His love in the bible and I'd even sung songs about it, but in this moment His love for me became real and tangible. Remember what I said to Jesus after He asked to be my first Valentine, "Great, but I'd have to do everything myself"! To be 127% honest, I didn't care what was in the goodie bag. I was just so moved that He led some woman to think of me, take action, go the store, and partner with Him to pick out a Valentine's Day gift for me. After more than a quarter of a century I finally had a Valentine! Jesus wasn't finished either. The next day I checked the mail as I routinely did and found a Valentine's Day card from my parents. This particular year it just happened to have a $25 gift card to a fancy seafood restaurant inside. Jesus wasn't kidding when He said He wanted to be my first Valentine, and the thing that got to me the most was that He was orchestrating the entire thing!

Valentine's Day finally arrived and I was finally included in the celebration! I woke up that morning overflowing with excitement. It was Valentine's Day and for the first time in my life I had a dinner date! Throughout the day my imagination ran wild with possibilities of what could be inside the gift. I left work in a hurry and headed home to get ready. I went all out getting ready, got dressed, called in my take out order, and jumped in the car to go pick it up. On my way home I felt prompted to stop by the supermarket, but I wasn't sure why. As I walked in the front doors I was immediately drawn to the flower section and was led to a bouquet of three pink long stemmed roses. I'd never been given flowers by a date before and Jesus had just ended my streak. I was so full of anticipation! I bought the roses and quickly headed home. My thoughts were racing. Was this real? Am I making this up? What was in the gift bag? When I got home I set the table and put the roses in a crystal vase. I turned on some worship music and sat down to enjoy my Valentine's "date" with Jesus. It was a picture perfect! My plate was full and so was my heart; bang bang shrimp, pink roses in a beautiful vase staring at me from the middle of the table, and a Valentine's

Day gift – for me – waiting to be opened! Actually, I didn't want to open it for two reasons. First, I was elated and content. I didn't care what was inside because the fact that I *had* a gift was enough for me. I was happy just sitting there enjoying my fancy dinner admiring my roses. Second, to be totally honest, I was nervous about finding out what was inside. I wondered what kind of gift would be inside the bag and I really didn't want to be disappointed. Finally, I decided that I wouldn't open it. A few minutes later I heard that still, small voice again, "Open it". Jesus was prodding me because He wanted to give me more. After wrestling through my thoughts of excitement and possible disappointment I decided to obey and I reached my hand in to see what was inside. The first thing I pulled out was a heart-shaped box of chocolates. The front of the box read "To My Princess". These words are nice and sweet for any Valentine, but the fact that my first name actually means "princess" took the experience to a much deeper level! Jesus was tenderly plucking the strings of my lonely heart and awakening me to my first love – Him. He was teaching me that He didn't just want me to have knowledge about Him, He wanted me to experience a relationship with Him!

Little did I know, but this Valentine encounter with Jesus was the beginning of a romance. The following year, Valentine's Day fell on a Sunday. I stood in the back of the sanctuary before the church service started and greeted people as they came in. I was fully engaged in a conversation with several women. When I realized it was Valentine's Day again, I noticed that the disheartening feeling I experienced the year before was gone. As I stood there talking, another woman approached me and handed me a gift bag. She told me that she was in a store a few days before and felt prompted to buy this gift for me and to give it to me on Valentine's Day. Once again, I didn't know or care what was in the bag, but I knew that Jesus, my Valentine, knew me and loved me. I thanked her and waited to open my gift at home where I could be alone with Jesus. When I got home, I immediately went to my bedroom and opened the gift. Inside was a clear tumbler with a pink lid that had "My Princess" written on the side. Wow, Jesus! This second woman had had no idea what had transpired the year before. Here I was again undone in His perfect love. Jesus sent me another Valentine the following year through a third woman from church – one single red rose and a card. None of these women knew what had happened previously, or was aware of how Jesus was weaving their obedience to His leading together to create our love story.

Through these Valentine encounters Jesus healed my heart and wooed me further and further into His. During this season, I also spent a lot of time reading Song of Solomon. I wanted my head knowledge of Jesus to somehow sink the eighteen inches it needed to go to become my heart knowledge of Jesus. As I read Song of Solomon over and over again, I was intrigued by the confidence in which the woman would speak about her Lover. In *Song of Solomon 1:5* the woman says, "Dark I am, yet lovely". I didn't understand how she could so confidently state that she was lovely. At times I hadn't felt very lovely, after all, and I hadn't been pursued or wooed in years. I wondered how this woman could believe she was lovely. I knew it was possible because I was reading about it in the bible, but I didn't have a clue how to get to a place where I could declare the same thing. My prayer became, "Jesus, whatever it takes. I want to be able to make that statement with the same level of confidence". Additionally, in Song of *Solomon 7:10* the woman confidently declares, "I am my Beloved's, His desire is for me". In comparing my beliefs against this scripture, I had accepted the truth that I belonged to Jesus. That made sense to me because He paid for my life on the cross. The second part of the verse was hard for me to swallow. I had no idea what it meant to be desired by a lover, so I read, re-read, prayed and asked Jesus to show me what He meant by these scriptures. It was these three Valentine's Day encounters and these revelations from Song of Solomon that were preparing me for something I had never considered or imagined!

My Takeaways From This Encounter
- Jesus loves me specifically and intentionally
- It's ok to share how I really feel with Jesus. It actually allows Him to be able to meet my needs and come through for me.
- Jesus will go to great lengths, even speak to others on my behalf, to demonstrate His great love
- My relationship with Jesus is real, not just words in a book or a story

Reflection

What is Jesus speaking to you through this encounter testimony?

_____

_____

_____

_____

_____

_____

_____

_____

Chapter 4
HEAVEN AT WORK

Encounter Testimony

After lunch one day I was walking down the hallway back to my office when a co-worker stopped and asked me for advice in taking care of some leg pain she was having. I had recently injured my foot and was currently in a walking boot so I guess she thought that I might have some insight. I found out that her pain level was pretty high and she was noticeably limping. I shared a few practical tips and told her that if she would come by my office I would pray for her leg if she wanted. She never stopped by that afternoon so I assumed she wasn't interested.

The next day she popped into my office just before 2pm. She just had a student cancel their meeting and wondered if I had time to pray for her. I had my own student meeting scheduled at 2pm and I told her we could pray quickly. I asked if I could put my hand on her calf where the pain was and she agreed. I literally prayed "pain leave" and asked her if it felt any better. The pain had gone down almost 50%! I asked her if I could pray again and she agreed. Again, I prayed "pain leave in Jesus name" and all the pain left from her leg! She thanked me and left the office. I received a text from her the next day sharing that the pain was still gone and she was able to go to the gym. She didn't come asking for prayer, but for advice for her injury. I took a risk in offering prayer and Jesus showed up at work!

My Takeaways From This Encounter
- I shouldn't ever assume people aren't open to prayer
- It's worth taking risks in order for someone to encounter Jesus
- Prayers don't have to be long to be effective
- People are watching my life and what I do each day matters

Reflection

What is Jesus speaking to you through this encounter testimony?

_____

_____

_____

_____

_____

_____

_____

_____

CHAPTER 5
HAPPY BIRTHDAY TO ME

Encounter Testimony

I walked into church that day as I normally did on Sunday mornings. We had some missionaries from Tanzania visiting and I had just celebrated my birthday the day before. I was catching up with and meeting new people that morning when a friend walked up and handed me a birthday present. The service was about to start so I thanked her and decided I would open it later. I got to my seat, put the gift under my chair, and entered into worship. Half way through worship, the Holy Spirit interrupted my singing and told me to open my gift.

I had already decided to open my birthday present after church, so when the thought came to mind I knew it was the Holy Spirit speaking to me. I've learned that good surprises are in store when the Holy Spirit interrupts my thoughts and this was one of those times. I quickly opened my birthday present to find a silver necklace with a shell pendant and a note from my friend. Her note wished me a happy birthday and included a verse she would be praying over me for the next year, *Ezekiel 37:1*. I'd read Ezekiel before, but I hadn't memorized the reference so I jumped onto the bible app on my phone and pulled up the reference, "The hand of the Lord was on me, and He brought me out by the Spirit of the Lord and set me in the middle of a valley; it was full of bones". Whoa, this was so good! I kept reading Ezekiel 37 through verse 10.

> *2 "He led me back and forth among them, and I saw a great many bones on the floor of the valley, bones that were very dry. 3 He asked me, "Son of man, can these bones live?" I said, "Sovereign Lord, you alone know."*
>
> *4 Then he said to me, "Prophesy to these bones and say to them, 'Dry bones, hear the word of the Lord! 5 This is what the Sovereign Lord says to these bones: I will make breath enter you, and you will come to life. 6 I will attach tendons to*

you and make flesh come upon you and cover you with skin;
I will put breath in you, and you will come to life. Then you
will know that I Am the Lord."'

7 So I prophesied as I was commanded. And as I was
prophesying, there was a noise, a rattling sound, and the bones
came together, bone to bone. 8 I looked, and tendons and flesh
appeared on them and skin covered them, but there was no
breath in them.

9 Then He said to me, "Prophesy to the breath; prophesy, son
of man, and say to it, 'This is what the Sovereign Lord says:
Come, breath, from the four winds and breathe into these
slain, that they may live.'" 10 So I prophesied as He
commanded me, and breath entered them; they came to life
and stood up on their feet—a vast army." (NIV)

After reading the Ezekiel passage I felt pretty encouraged. I put the card and gift back in the bag, slid it back under my seat, and entered back into worship. Worship ended and Mary Street, the missionary from Tanzania, got up to preach. She introduced her family, shared a mission update, and then told us to turn to Ezekiel 37. She then proceeded to read verses one through ten of Ezekiel 37 – the exact verses, in the exact book, out of the entire sixty-six books of the bible that I had literally just read! The tears just started rolling down my cheeks as Holy Spirit started speaking to me.

My Takeaways From This Encounter
- He cares enough to orchestrate the details of someone bringing me a birthday present the day after my birthday, the missionaries being at church the day I was given the birthday present, and speaking to both women about Ezekiel 37
- I want to obey Him even when I don't understand why He's asking me to do something
- Jesus does a good job of loving me and cares about the details of my life

Reflection

What is Jesus speaking to you through this encounter testimony?

_____

_____

_____

_____

_____

_____

_____

_____

CHAPTER 6

THE BIG QUESTION

Encounter Testimony

While working at a campus ministry at Florida State University, I lived one block from the edge of campus. If you have never visited Florida State's campus, it's absolutely beautiful! The campus is lined with stunning traditional red brick buildings and many of the sidewalks are often canopied by spreading oak trees. There are flowers planted throughout campus that offer delightful colors of pinks, purples, reds, and blues. There old fashioned street lamps to light the way and statues of men and women who helped shape the university's mission over the years. In the four years I lived at the campus ministry, I often took walks around campus to spend time with Jesus. On my walks with Him I would most often ask questions and then spend time listening to His answers. As we walked and talked I would imagine Him walking beside me, jumping over puddles, walking in the dirt as we took a narrower path, and sitting next to me when I stopped at one of the many benches to gaze at the clouds dancing across the sky.

I thoroughly enjoyed dating Jesus, but the pursuit He began with the Valentine's Day encounter was about to turn into full blown romance. I continued going on dates with Him almost weekly. Spending time with Jesus outside held a special place in my heart because of that very first encounter I had with Him watching the sunrise at Pretty Place. On one particular day, I started my walk by laying on a bench next to the Westcott fountain. It was fall and there was a cool breeze and the sky was a beautiful deep blue. I read my bible and spent time admiring creation. After a while I decided to continue my walk. I headed towards the heart of campus passing by the reflection pond and several beds of flowers. I turned right near the old Psychology building and headed down the sidewalk past the School of Music, all the while praying and asking questions. As I spent time with Jesus that day nothing particularly profound or revelatory had happened, it was a typical prayer walk. I crossed the street and stopped next to a statue of Claude Pepper, a Florida Senator, to admire the beauty of the sky, completely unaware of what was about to happen. Remember, one moment in His presence can change everything and little did I know I was about to experience one of those moments. As I stood there admiring the clouds, I heard His familiar still, small voice inside my head, "Will you marry me?" All my thoughts screeched to a halt. What did He just say? I heard Him again, "Will you marry me?". Instantly, almost like a reflex, my heart spoke before my brain could catch up and I replied, "Yes, I will marry you". Jesus spoke again, something else I wasn't expecting and something that was rather terrifying to me, "I want you to get a ring and wear it". I was surprised at what Jesus had just asked of me. My heart brimmed with excitement at the idea and I was terrified of His request to wear a ring. I never wore jewelry on a consistent basis before because I had always been playing some type of sport and sports and jewelry do not go well together. I also knew that wearing jewelry would draw attention which would lead to questioning. At that point in my life, I wasn't too keen on the idea of doing anything that caused me to be noticed. In hindsight, I was actually hiding my beauty as some twisted form of self protection. From what? I'm not sure, but at that point in my life I would have preferred not to wear a ring. On the other hand, Jesus was worth anything I had to get over within me, so I chose to move forward and agree to wear a ring.

Despite the excitement I felt in my heart it took me several days to get up the courage to go look for a ring. I decided I would go to the mall and look for a silver ring. I'd never picked out a ring and I wasn't about to ask anyone to come with me to buy a wedding ring. I stopped at a kiosk in the middle of the mall and looked at all the silver rings with Jesus to see which one was highlighted. We finally settled on a silver band that had a dove-shaped cutout. I paid for the ring and left the mall hoping no one had seen me. When I got in the car I was still struggling with the thought of wearing jewelry. I didn't mind wearing it as a symbol of our marriage covenant, but I dreaded the possibility of being asked about my new fashion statement. Despite my nervousness, I decided to put the ring on my left ring finger and hope no one noticed. The only problem with wearing it on my left hand is that rings on the left ring finger are engagement rings in the United States. Jesus had asked me to marry Him and I was afraid to put the ring on the correct hand indicating marriage. The even bigger problem was that I was letting fear influence my obedience to what He had asked of me.

I arrived back at my apartment wearing my new wedding ring and my worst fear came true, in less than two minutes one of my roommates began to ask questions about the ring. I quickly informed her that I got it at the mall which didn't seem to satisfy her curiosity and followed up with more questions as to why I had purchased the ring in the first place. My worst fears were coming true and it had been less two minutes! How was I going to explain that Jesus asked me to marry Him and to get a ring and wear it? Well, that was the only explanation I had so that's what I said. She mentioned how she thought it was cool and finally left me alone.

It took a few weeks before I felt convicted enough to put the ring on my right hand, but Jesus lovingly continued to romance me through His Word and our conversations. I was learning what it truly meant to be the bride of Christ!

My Takeaways From This Encounter
- Jesus wasn't kidding when He invited me to be the Bride of Christ
- Jesus really wants to be one with me
- Fear of man and shame can keep me from being fully obedient to Him
- When spending time with Jesus He can surprise me at any moment

Reflection
What is Jesus speaking to you through this encounter testimony?

_____

_____

_____

_____

_____

_____

_____

_____

CHAPTER 7
LOVE NEVER FAILS

Encounter Testimony

I recently attended an Iris Global conference led by main speakers Heidi Baker and Will Hart. It was the second day of the conference and we had just finished a session hearing amazing stories of supernatural healing, provision, and miracles. I was eating Chick-fil-a on our lunch break with a group of friends when a man, we'd later learn was named Johnny, came in the store. He was handing something out as he visited each of the tables. He got to our table and placed a woven leather key chain in front of me with a tag that read, "I'm deaf. Please help support me by giving $3-$5. Thank you". My friend at the end of the table leaned over and suggested that we pray for him and I agreed.

I caught his attention and motioned to ask if I could pray for him. He agreed. Next I asked his name and by reading his lips discovered it was Johnny. Remember, we had just left a conference session hearing testimonies of deaf ears opening. How could I not pray?!?! I commanded his ears to open in Jesus name while snapping my fingers near his right ear to see if anything was changing. Nothing, but that's ok. The point isn't healing, the point is loving well. I put my hand on his back and released the love of the Father over him. He immediately began laughing and it was obvious that joy was bubbling up inside of Johnny. Next I put my hand on his heart and continued to release the love of the Father asking Holy Spirit to fill him up. I stopped praying, Johnny hugged me, signed I love you, and continued to the next table. My friend bought him a meal. He hugged her and left the store. His hearing may not have been healed that day, but I know he experienced the love of Jesus.

My Takeaways From This Encounter
- Healing doesn't always happen, but love is always possible
- I will continue to take risks even when I don't see the miracle

- When the rubber meets the road I actually acted on what I say I believe
- It's not failure if I have loved well

Reflection

What is Jesus speaking to you through this encounter testimony?

_____

_____

_____

_____

_____

_____

_____

_____

CHAPTER 8
DANCING IN THE GARDEN

Encounter Testimony

In my limited understanding of unconditional love, my first encounter with Jesus on Valentine's Day would have sufficed. Jesus, however, is Love; and what came next, once again, I could have never imagined. In the spring of 2012, I was serving as the head of the chapel at a women's retreat called Tres Dias. The retreat is structured as a three-day encounter with Jesus and this particular weekend's theme was "That I May Dwell, Face to Face". Each Tres Dias retreat includes a weekend song, weekend scripture, and weekend theme. During this retreat the weekend song was "Show Me Your Glory". The weekend theme was a bride in a white wedding dress standing in front of a waterfall with the Holy Spirit as a dove hovering in front of and over her head. As the head of the chapel, it was my responsibility to oversee the functions and details for all the chapel services during the weekend. I had served in the chapel before and felt well-prepared to lead the team in the duties of set up, communion, and music. The woman leading the entire weekend requested that the chapel put on an ongoing drama throughout the weekend as the attendees entered and left the chapel. She charged me, as Head Chapel, to pray, create, and plan a skit that would progress throughout the weekend using a list of songs she had picked. I had no idea how Jesus had been using this position and theme to set me up for another encounter with Him!

I began praying and asking Jesus for a vision for the skit. He began to show me a series of scenes of a girl wearing a t-shirt with the word "REJECTED" taped on the front and back. Jesus showed me a series of scenes, using the songs that would transform the girl from rejected into His Bride standing in front of the waterfall with the dove hovering overhead. Part of my job as Head Chapel was to assign different tasks to the people on my team, one of which was to decide who was going to play the girl in the skit. The more I prayed the more I felt like I was the one who was supposed to play the girl. I struggled with accepting the role because I was afraid it wasn't suitable for me, as the leader, to choose myself. After discussing it with the retreat leader I realized that I wasn't choosing myself, but instead being obedient.

Before preparations for the weekend were underway, Jesus had already been setting me up to play the girl in the skit. I just had not yet connected all the dots. For weeks when I was driving to and from work this bridal shop sign would be highlighted to me. Holy Spirit would focus my attention onto the sign every time I drove by. The sign was pink, which was not one of my favorite colors at the time, and it was a bridal shop and I wasn't anywhere close to needing their services! After accepting the role in the skit, I began searching for a wedding dress to use for the final scene as the bride in front of the waterfall. One would think that with over one hundred women serving on the weekend, someone would have a wedding dress that I could borrow for the dance we were doing at the culmination of the skit. Nope! Not one woman had a wedding dress that would work. Meanwhile, my church had a worship night that I attended which was not connected to the retreat. That night as I walked around the sanctuary worshiping and enjoying God's presence, I suddenly realized that I had just walked down the middle aisle of the church. You know, the aisle that all brides walk down?! As soon as I had that thought and it registered in my brain I heard Jesus ask me, "Can I have the first dance?" What?! How could that even be possible? My brain finally caught up to what was happening and I knew immediately that He was referring to the dance at the end of the skit, when the rejected girl becomes His Bride!

The dots slowly connected – seeing the bridal shop sign for weeks, no one had a dress I could borrow, needing a wedding dress specifically for the skit – this was more than a skit for a retreat. This was an invitation for me to be His Bride publically. I also sensed that He was leading me to buy a dress. So many questions surfaced. How will I know which one to pick out? Who is crazy enough to believe me and go with me to pick one out? How much is this going to cost? Am I crazy? It was a mix of exciting, scary, wonderful and vulnerable. I eventually decided to ask a friend who I knew would be willing to step out of the proverbial boat with me as she had recently gotten married. Dress shopping day finally arrived and we met up at a local bridal shop. My plan was to get one of those $99 dresses, but soon found out they weren't running that special anymore. Next we tried the mall and searched every department store hoping to find something at a reasonable price. There weren't any suitable wedding dresses in any store. We stopped by a boutique my friend tried when she was dress shopping; nothing there either. Then it dawned on me that maybe, just maybe, I would find my wedding dress at the bridal shop with the familiar pink sign that had been highlighted for months. We arrived at the pink-signed shop and the owner met us at the door asking us how she could help. I told her my size and she said she had several options. This was the first store that had any viable options. As I tried on the dress she stood outside the dressing room and asked the typical questions - Who is the lucky man? When is the wedding date? I didn't know what else to do other than tell the truth. She shared that she was also Christian and she thought the idea was wonderful. The first dress I tried on was too big, but the second dress fit perfectly! I bought it, thanked the woman and my friend, and eagerly waited for the retreat weekend to come.

I was excited to lead the chapel and the entire skit as a whole, but I was in no way prepared for the intensity or magnitude of the encounter I was about to experience. The weekend started on a Thursday night as we kicked off the skit at the evening chapel. I was dressed as the girl, wearing the rejected t-shirt, standing in front of a mirror as the song "The Real Me" by Natalie Grant played:

Foolish heart looks like we're here again
Same old game of plastic smile don't let anybody in
Hiding my heartache, will this glass house break
How much will they take before I'm empty
Do I let it show, does anybody know?

But you see the real me hiding in my skin, broken from within
Unveil me completely I'm loosening my grasp
There's no need to mask my frailty
'Cause you see the real me

Painted on, life is behind a mask
Self-inflicted circus clown I'm tired of the song and dance
Living a charade, always on parade
What a mess I've made of my existence
But you love me even now and still I see somehow

But you see the real me hiding in my skin, broken from within
Unveil me completely I'm loosening my grasp

There's no need to mask my frailty
'Cause you see the real me

Wonderful, beautiful is what you see
When you look at me
You're turning the tattered fabric of my life into
A perfect tapestry I just wanna be me

But you see the real me hiding in my skin, broken from within
Unveil me completely I'm loosening my grasp
There's no need to mask my frailty
'Cause you see the real me and you love me just as I am
Wonderful, beautiful is what you see when you look at me

Half way through the song it dawned on me that I wasn't just playing a role in the skit, but I *was* the girl in the skit. The words to that song are a pretty accurate description how any woman has felt at some point, but what started that night in front of the mirror was a deep healing in my heart.

The next night, during Friday's evening chapel scene, I came in wearing the rejected t-shirt and dancing with a huge flag to a song of victory. In Saturday morning's chapel, the girl was to sit on a bench next to a wisteria tree and read her bible as the candidates came in and out of the chapel. At the Saturday afternoon chapel, the retreat leader revealed the theme and song for the weekend. The weekend song was introduced by having the worship team play it for the candidates. The scene for that chapel had the girl coming up the stairs into the room and walking down the center aisle towards the cross while pretending to cry out for more of God. The song started playing and I heard my cue to start coming up the stairs. My foot hit the floor as I entered the chapel, and when the worship leader belted out the line in the song, "I'm not afraid," I began walking up to the cross. I wasn't more than two steps in before my pretend crying out for more of God became real - and my own tears soon streamed down my face. Yes, I was the girl in the mirror that had been hiding. Yes, I wanted to see more of His glory. I was a beautiful mess!

The scenes continued to come as each chapel rolled around, and I began to not merely play a role, but be the role. Jesus used the skit to reveal and heal things in my heart that I did not even know existed. During another Saturday chapel, I had been positioned in a still scene sitting on a blanket reading my bible. As soon as they were all inside and the door was closed, I threw on my sweatshirt and came through a side door to run the sound board during worship. I wore my sweatshirt because I was still wearing the rejected t-shirt and would soon need to run out the side door and get back on blanket to read my bible when chapel was over. During worship I put my hand over my heart and Jesus began to speak to me, "Why do you let rejection get in between you and Me?" I could feel the tape underneath my sweatshirt between my hand and my heart that said "REJECTED". Jesus tried to show me how much He loved me, but in order to receive that, I had to stop accepting rejection. Even after my Valentine's Day encounter and Jesus asking me to marry Him, I still struggled with some unbelief and a feeling of rejection. I realized that I am not alone in having felt this. This is nothing new, as the enemy uses the same tactics on everyone, just in different ways, different settings, and using different circumstances.

Later that same evening, an opportunity presented itself to forgive anyone we may need to forgive. We were all instructed to write down the names of those we needed to forgive on a red heart. The hearts were nailed to a cross and then taken out to a fire pit to be burned. It was in that moment that I chose to give up any feelings of rejection and I burned the rejected t-shirt in the fire that night. The next morning was Sunday, the last part of the skit and the part where the girl becomes the bride. There were several married ladies on my team who helped me get dressed and ready for the final scene of the skit. It was time for the first dance Jesus had asked for during the worship night at the front of the church. This time, I was dressed and ready to dance with my Beloved. The song "Garden" by Misty Edwards began to play as I walked down the stairs as His bride in my beautiful white wedding dress, no longer rejected, and danced.

> *It's You and me alone God You and me alone*
> *Here it's You and me alone God You and me alone*
>
> *You've hedged me in with skin all around me*
> *I'm a garden enclosed a locked garden*
> *Life takes place behind the face.*
>
> *So come into Your garden*
> *Come into Your garden.*

Here O Lord! Have I prepared a place for You!

I'm no longer my own I'm Your garden

I don't want to waste my time living on the outside
I'm going to live from the inside out
I don't want to waste my life living on the outside
I'm going to live from the inside out

I can honestly say, I was so caught up in His presence I was completely unaware of all the candidates and team that stood in a semicircle around me. For them it was the final part of a skit, but for me it was our *first dance, or better yet,* our *wedding dance*! It has been several years since that first dance and I can confidently say that I am still in love with Jesus and He is still romancing me. As I write my story, I am enjoying a weeklong vacation with my Beloved. It is just the two of us and that is all I need. It may seem extreme to some, but I am serious about cultivating my relationship with Him. I want to know Him and be known by Him. The truth I found is that Jesus wants an intimate marriage-like relationship with each of us. I pray that you are inspired by my testimony, but the best is yet to come!

My Takeaways From This Encounter
- Getting caught up in His presence is the most amazing experience ever
- There is something vulnerable and beautiful and freeing about dancing
- He will do immeasurably more than I could ever ask or imagine

Reflection
What is Jesus speaking to you through this encounter testimony?

_____

_____

_____

_____

_____

_____

CHAPTER 9
JUST A MOMENT

Encounter Testimony

I was the Program Coordinator for a grant at Tallahassee Community College. The grant funded a peer leadership program and I was in charge of training and mentoring the Peer Leaders who were then placed in classrooms to assist professors. It was the second semester of the program and our Peer Leaders had grown from eight to twenty-four. The entire program was housed in my office which included desk space for myself, the Assistant Program Coordinator, and up to three or four Peer Leaders at a time. That said, my office was often chaotic as we launched and built the program simultaneously.

On this particular day one of the Peer Leaders had called in sick. It didn't seem out of the ordinary since something had been going around. I texted her back thanking her for letting me know and hoping she felt better soon. The day progressed as planned with meetings, conference calls, scheduling, and answering questions as the Peer Leaders came in and out of the office. Around two o'clock I had five minutes to sit at my desk between meetings and the thought popped into my head that I should check on my Peer Leader. I gave her a quick call, asked her how she was feeling, found out she was doing better, and told her I would see her in the morning. She showed up the next morning and carried out her responsibilities as usual. Two weeks later she came into the office, sat me down, and shared something that has impacted me ever since. She shared that right when I called to check on her that day she was about to end her life. Jesus! It wasn't normal for me to call to check on students that called in sick, but in that five-minute window of sitting at my desk I was aware of His voice and obeyed.

My Takeaways From This Encounter
- It's so important to act on what I hear Jesus speaking to me
- Jesus will use anyone who is willing to tune in and be obedient

- Jesus really loves people. He cared enough to prompt me to act on behalf of another.
- I don't have to understand to act and sometimes I'm glad I don't know the weight of the situation

Reflection

What is Jesus speaking to you through this encounter testimony?

_____

_____

_____

_____

_____

_____

_____

_____

CHAPTER 10

SUPERNATURAL CODING

Encounter Testimony

A friend who works in IT shared this post on her Facebook page, "Does anyone know VBA? I have a piece of code I'm fighting with and would love some help if you can spare the time". I was walking across campus to get some coffee when I read her post and thought it would be fun to ask Holy Spirit for a word of knowledge to fix her coding problem. Here is my friend's account of our interaction from her blog post:

As hour four quickly closed, I felt no closer to figuring out how to write a particular piece of application code that my supervisor wanted than when I first started. I admit to feeling a little hopeless at that point. I may be in the computer field, but I am not a programmer. I stared at the code with frustration for a long minute.

"Ask me," the Lord stirred within in my heart in that familiar still, small voice.

"Okay," I responded obediently, unsure what to ask exactly. "Lord, will you point me to the right resource?"

A few minutes after hearing nothing more, I texted a friend who knew the code language that I needed (I laugh now as I write this post because I think I felt like I needed to help the Lord answer my prayer). My friend tried to help and pointed me to a couple of sites, but my particular code issue was not something he was familiar with writing. The sites were useful suggestions, but after another hour fiddling with the code, I realized I was getting nowhere fast. As a last resort, I used my lunch to post a plea to Facebook for help.

"Now, what do I do, Lord?" I sighed. A minute later, my smart phone buzzed with a message from another friend who responded to my request for help.

"Did you ask the Holy Spirit about the code?" my friend asked.

"I asked Him for a solution," I wrote back quickly.

"I agree He'll lead you to a solution. I'm asking for a word of knowledge about it. I have no idea in the natural [physical world]. I'll let you know what I hear in a few minutes."

About ten minutes later, I received a follow-up message from my friend, "There's something in the second part of the code. Does that make sense at all?"

I went back to my original code and started at the second sub statement, which happened to be the part I was struggling with all morning. Knowing that she had not seen the code and wasn't a programmer, I started laughing at my excitement at what the Lord was doing through her, "Yes, your response makes perfect sense! I still need to get clarification on what to do with the second part though."

"Okay, I didn't know if codes have parts. LOL! I'll ask what to do with it," she confirmed before shortly continuing a minute later, "Delete something is what I heard. Like there's too much maybe?" she mentioned.

I instantly recognized what she meant. "Yes, I think I did add too much to my code," I agreed.

Although my friend could not hear me, I was laughing again as I looked at the code and removed what I suspected was incorrect from the overall module. When I was done making changes, I eagerly tested the code, but encountered an error. However, I remained determined and I felt in my spirit that we were on the right path.

"I have no idea what I'm talking about," my friend texted.

"That is funny to me, because I do know what you're saying," I confirmed. "I deleted the problematic code, but something is still missing."

"Okay, I'm asking," she responded and quickly followed up with "I am hearing something about a closing statement. Do they have those in programming?"

"Yes, closing statements are in programming" I confirmed.

I scrolled to the last closing statement, but nothing looked wrong. Everything appeared to be in order, and the syntax appeared correct. While I was still searching for my mistake, I received another message from my friend.

"Maybe not in the closing closing statement but one further up in the code?" she urged without knowing I was still struggling.

Her words suddenly made sense. Of course, the issue was with the end sub statement at the tail-end of the second sub command. It was the same code I had wrestled with all day. Immediately, I found the syntax error and corrected it. My fingers couldn't press the run button fast enough when I realized that error was likely the last barrier to making the code work. Believe it or not, it worked!

Perfectly! Only God could do that. I am still in awe.

(Blog post by Heather White, www.loveroars.com)

I was just as amazed that He would speak to me in such a specific way. After all, Jesus is the Way, the Truth, and the Life and what a privilege it is to be able to access His resurrection power bringing Heaven to earth.

My Takeaways From This Encounter

- Everything matters to Jesus
- When I ask I really can receive answers that I need
- Taking risks allows me to experience the supernatural in my every day life
- Partnering with Jesus is FUN!

Reflection

What is Jesus speaking to you through this encounter testimony?

_____

_____

_____

_____

_____

_____

_____

_____

30 DAY PRACTICAL GUIDE

CHAPTER 11

PREPARING FOR YOUR ENCOUNTER JOURNEY

It is now time for you to begin cultivating new levels of awareness and intimacy through encounters with Jesus. In the second part of the book you will find a thirty-day encounter journey for you to take with Jesus. There are no rules to follow or parameters to stay within. Remember, this is *your* relationship with Jesus and you have the freedom to change, modify, and adapt these encounters to meet *your* needs. Think of these encounter activations as a starting point for taking you deeper in your relationship with Jesus. From that point, run with it in a manner that suits your relationship with Jesus.

Before you begin your thirty-day encounter journey with Jesus, I want to share several permission statements with you. Take a few minutes to speak these over yourself. You may even want to stand up as you declare them. I've often found that physical demonstrations, just like raising your hands in worship, kneeling in prayer, or standing can be prophetic acts of agreement. Also, feel free to create your own permission statements. These are designed to help you prepare your heart and mind as you move into the encounter activation portion of this experience. Remember, Jesus wants to know you and be known by you. He's ready and waiting to meet you wherever, whenever, and however you come!

Permission Statements
- I give myself permission to have needs.
- I give myself permission to share raw, unfiltered thoughts with Jesus.
- I give myself permission to share raw, unfiltered feelings with Jesus.
- I give myself permission to have desires.
- I give myself permission to be fully loved by Jesus.
- I give myself permission to have fun.

Write Your Own Permission Statements

- _____
- _____
- _____
- _____
- _____

Share Your Encounter Testimonies

As you go through this thirty-day encounter journey with Jesus I'd love to celebrate what He is doing in your life by sharing your encounter testimonies through the beENCOUNTERed website (*www.beENCOUNTERed.com*) and Facebook page (*@beENCOUNTERed*).

Testimonies can also be emailed to sarah@beencountered.com.

CHAPTER 12

FIVE KEYS FOR ENCOUNTERING JESUS

I so enjoy sharing the encounters that I've had with Jesus, but I'm even more excited to shift our focus onto deepening your experiences encountering Jesus! Below are five keys that will help you on your journey. These are the things that I wish I had known early on, but discovered along the way. If you have any doubts about your relationship with Jesus or hearing His voice, I ask that you trust me now and believe me later. I promise He won't let you down. You only need faith as small as a mustard seed, and if you've read this far I am confident that you have enough faith to grow stronger and go deeper in your relationship with Him!

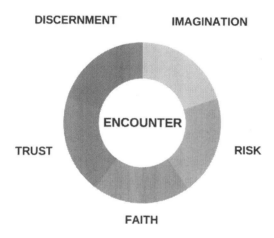

Key #1: Discernment

The first key I discovered encountering Jesus is being able to discern whose voice you are hearing. There are three possible choices – His, ours, or the enemy. The easiest voice to filter out is that of the enemy. *Romans 8:1* teach us that, "Therefore, there is now no condemnation for those who are in Christ Jesus". This truth is a proven filter for discerning what voice you are hearing. If what you hear is negative, discouraging, disapproving, or condemning in anyway you can be sure, according to *Romans 8:1*, that it isn't Jesus speaking. *Proverbs 18:21* teaches us that "the tongue has the power of life and death". That is, our words have power and that power will either bring death or life to the situation. Combining the truths in Romans 8:1 and Proverbs 18:21 we can check the fruit of the words that we are hearing. If we are hearing words that bring death and condemnation they come from the enemy. Conversely, if we hear words that are bringing us life and encouragement then they are from Jesus.

Discerning the two remaining voices, His and ours, has been more of a process for me. Again, scripture is the best filter to measure what you are hearing. Once the enemy is ruled out, what was heard can now be tested to see if it agrees with scripture. If it doesn't agree then it can be ruled out. If it does agree, then it's time to test what you've heard against your own beliefs. Another way that I've learned to know if Jesus is speaking is when I hear something I would have never thought of myself. For example, when Jesus asked me to marry Him it was a thought that had never crossed my mind. As I filtered His request through scripture I concluded that it was in agreement with scripture and chose to move forward in the encounter. Using scripture to filter what we are hearing definitely enables us to discern the voice of God more clearly.

Key #2: Imagination

The second key I discovered encountering Jesus is using our imagination to connect with and encounter Him. In *Ephesians 3:20* we are encouraged to ask and imagine because God "is able to do immeasurably more than all we ask or imagine". Additionally, in *1 Corinthians 2:16* we are told that "we have the mind of Christ". This reveals the truth that we have been given a sanctified mind and, therefore, can encounter Jesus in and through our sanctified imagination. These encounter experiences through imagination can also be described as seeing something in your mind's eye or seeing or feeling something in your spirit. When we trust in the truths found in scripture, the realm of possibility opens up to "immeasurably more" than we ask or imagine. Subsequently, as we encounter Jesus through our imagination He will do immeasurably more than anything we ask or imagine!

In *John 1* we find Jesus in the process of calling His disciples. In *John 1:47* He sees Nathaniel approaching and says to him, "Here truly is an Israelite in whom there is no deceit". Nathaniel, having never met Jesus, responds in confusion and wonder asking Jesus to explain how He knew him. Jesus replied, "I saw you while you were still under the fig tree before Philip called you". Jesus saw Nathaniel before He actually saw Nathaniel in person. We have been given access to see by the Spirit in the spiritual realm before we see something in the natural realm!

Key #3: Risk

The third key I discovered encountering Jesus is taking risks. Risk taking gets us outside our comfort zones and stretches us to grow. The bible is full of testimonies of people taking risks in their relationships with Jesus that resulted in supernatural encounters. Peter stepped out of the boat at Jesus' invitation. Peter's risk of stepping out of the boat allowed him to experience walking on water. Servants filled stone jars with water at Jesus' command. Their obedience resulted in witnessing water turned to wine. The woman who had been bleeding for 12 years pushed her way through the crowd and touched the hem of Jesus' garment. Her risk led to her healing. Peter did not know what would happen when he stepped out of the boat. The servants had never seen water turned into wine. No one had been able to help the woman. As they encountered Jesus they took risks through simple actions. Their faith combined with His presence and power produced supernatural encounters that transformed their lives.

In *John 14:12* Jesus tells us, "whoever believes in Me will do the works I have been doing, and they will do even greater things than these". The "greater works" are for us too! We can experience God's presence and power in us and through us by taking risks just like Peter and the others did. A few years ago I had a friend who had been asked to lead worship at a funeral for a man from our church. She woke up the morning of the funeral with a migraine that was severe enough to make her sick. I had been reading the biography of John G. Lake, a leader in the divine healing movement, who operated in the gifts of faith and healing. Inspired by his healing testimonies, I decided to take a risk and pray for my friend. I spoke to the migraine and commanded it to leave in Jesus name. After praying that prayer several times all the pain and nausea were gone! This is one of many stories that continue to encourage me to give Jesus the opportunity to flow through me by stepping out and taking risks.

Key #4: Faith

The fourth key I discovered encountering Jesus is faith. *Hebrews 11:1* describes faith, "Now faith is being sure of what we hope for and certain of what we do not see". Are you *sure* that Jesus wants to meet you in your hopes? Are you *certain* of the things you are believing for, but have yet to see in the natural? Lacking faith will definitely make it more difficult to encounter Jesus and experience what He is saying and doing in our lives. The good news is that we can build our faith *through* encountering Jesus. We are promised in *Romans 10:17* that, "faith comes by hearing, and hearing by the word of God" and *John 1:14* reveals that "the Word became flesh and dwelt among us". Jesus is the Word. Therefore, we can begin to encounter Jesus by the measure of faith we already have and as we encounter Him and hear from Him, our faith will grow!

Finally, in *Ephesians 2:6* we are promised, "God raised us up with Christ and seated us with Him in the heavenly realms in Christ Jesus". We can access this truth through our faith and live our lives from Heaven to earth. It is our faith in the person of Truth, Jesus, that shifts our reality, allowing us to encounter Jesus – everything He wants to say and do *in* and *through* and *for* us.

Key #5: Trust

The fifth key I discovered encountering Jesus is trusting that He wants to connect and be in relationship with us individually. Jesus died to redeem the relational connection that was lost through sin. We now have access to a relationship with Him because of His sacrifice. As with any close relationship, communication is essential and to communicate we must have some level of trust in order to receive the speaker and their message. We only have two choices, trust or mistrust. We must trust that He is speaking and have faith in the truths revealed through scripture in order to receive the benefits of relationship that Jesus purchased for us on the cross. *Jeremiah 33:3*, "Call to Me and I will answer you and tell you great and unsearchable things you do not know", promises that as we call He will answer. *John 10:27*, "My sheep hear My voice, and I know them, and they follow Me", gives evidence that, as His sheep, we hear His voice. We can either doubt the truth of the Word of God or we can choose to trust and believe. We must choose to trust and believe in order to encounter Jesus. *James 4:8* promises, "Come near to God and he will come near to you". When we choose to come into His presence with trust believing that He wants to speak to us and open our hearts to receive truth it allows Jesus to do "immeasurably more than we can ask or imagine" (*Ephesians 3:20*).

I am thankful for these keys I've discovered along the way as I've spent time encountering Jesus and it is my honor and privilege to pass them along to you. May my ceiling be your floor!

CHAPTER 13
YOUR INVITATION

Beloved,

I have been waiting to spend this time with you and I AM delighted it has finally arrived! I love how much you love Me. I love that you want to spend more time with Me and I love that you are opening up yourself, setting aside this time, and seeking more of Me.

I want you to know that I AM not a formula to figure out. I AM not a set of rules that you need to follow. I AM not beyond your reach. I AM not unaware of your humanity. I understand you. I see you. I consider everything that you do. I do these things not to judge you – judgment was resolved on the cross – but because I want to know you. I want to know the real, authentic you – not any masked version of you or the perfected version of you – but the raw and real and most unfiltered you that you have to offer. The real you is the you that I want to spend time with! That is the you that I want to know! That is the you that I love!

Know that I do not expect anything from you. I just want to spend time with you and lavish you with My unconditional love over and over and over again.

Will you let Me?

I've Made You Worthy,
Jesus

CHAPTER 14
INVITING JESUS INTO
YOUR DAILY ROUTINE

I don't know about you, but for a long time my mentality was that quality time with Jesus had to be an uninterrupted long amount of time. Anything less than thirty minutes felt like a failure. I've since learned that Jesus is way more practical than that and really just wants to be with us, doing life together. I've also learned that some of my most intimate encounters with Jesus have come while doing some of the most mundane tasks in life. I have lost count of how many encounters I've had just running errands with Jesus. Doing life with Him is so AMAZING!

We can live naturally supernatural in the context of every day life! Jesus was fully God and fully man. His life shows us how to live naturally supernatural. Yes, we see Jesus praying, healing the sick, and sharing the Good News, but He also did human things like eating, sleeping, and even worked as a carpenter. I encourage you to view this thirty-day journey of encounter activations, which has come from my personal experiences, as an opportunity for deepening your relationship with Jesus.

ENCOUNTER JESUS:
DAY 1

Activation
Brush your teeth with Jesus.

Instructions
Use this time to listen to what Jesus wants to share with you.

Reflection
Describe this encounter with Jesus.

_____

_____

_____

_____

_____

What did you like/dislike about encountering Jesus while brushing your teeth?

_____

_____

_____

_____

_____

What is one way you experienced Jesus in a new way?

_____

_____

_____

_____

_____

Takeaways From This Encounter With Jesus

ENCOUNTER JESUS:
DAY 2

Activation
Shift atmospheres with Jesus.

Instructions
Colors have prophetic meaning (visit www.beENCOUNTERed.com/colors for a guide to the prophetic meaning of color). Ask Jesus to highlight which colors to wear today. Stay aware of your environments as you go throughout the day to see the affect of what He is releasing through your prophetic act.

Reflection
What differences did you observe in your atmospheres today (home, work, school, gym, etc.)?

_____

_____

_____

_____

_____

What revelation did you gain from this encounter with Jesus?

_____

_____

_____

_____

_____

What is a one way you want to integrate the prophetic meaning of color into every day life?

_____

_____

_____

_____

_____

Takeaways From This Encounter With Jesus

ENCOUNTER JESUS:
DAY 3

Activation
Eat breakfast with Jesus.

Instructions
Invite Jesus to join you for breakfast, regardless if you're sitting down enjoy the meal or running out the door with a protein bar. Take advantage of the small moments you have to connect to Jesus. Ask Him what is on His heart for today.

Reflection
Do you find it easy or hard to connect with Jesus in your daily routine?

_____

_____

_____

_____

_____

What do you think/feel knowing the Savior of the world wants to have breakfast with you?

_____

_____

_____

_____

_____

What did Jesus reveal to you through this encounter?

_____

_____

_____

_____

_____

Takeaways From This Encounter With Jesus

ENCOUNTER JESUS:
DAY 4

Activation
On the go with Jesus.

Instructions
Spend time talking with Jesus as you travel from place to place today. Use the five minutes in the car, the walk to the mailbox, biking to class, etc. to spend time with Jesus.

Reflection
What was one thing Jesus shared with you that you weren't expecting?

_____

_____

_____

_____

_____

What was easy about connecting with Jesus during this encounter? Why?

_____

_____

_____

_____

_____

What was difficult about connecting with Jesus during this encounter? Why?

_____

_____

_____

_____

_____

Takeaways From This Encounter With Jesus

ENCOUNTER JESUS:
DAY 5

Activation
Work with Jesus.

Instructions
You may be a top level executive, stay at home mom, student, or retired...
today invite Jesus to join you in whatever you consider your "work" to be.
Ask for divine strategies and wisdom for your work.

Reflection
What strategies did Jesus reveal to you today as you worked together?

_____

_____

_____

_____

_____

What other area of life would you like to invite Jesus into in a similar way?

_____

_____

_____

_____

What is one thing you can implement with Jesus in your work moving
forward?

_____

_____

_____

_____

Takeaways From This Encounter With Jesus

ENCOUNTER JESUS:
DAY 6

Activation
Eat lunch with Jesus.

Instructions
Whether you eat at home, pack it, or go out to lunch, bring your bible and spend time conversing with Jesus today. Jesus is the Word made flesh (*John 1:14*). Ask Him a question and then ask Him for a verse reference. If the verse you get doesn't make sense, just try again. There is grace!

Reflection
How has this encounter impacted your relationship with Jesus?

_____

_____

_____

_____

_____

What verse impacted you the most during this encounter with Jesus?

_____

_____

_____

_____

What other questions do you have for Jesus?

_____

_____

_____

_____

Takeaways From This Encounter With Jesus

ENCOUNTER JESUS:
DAY 7

Activation
Take a break with Jesus.

Instructions
As you take a break from your day, invite Jesus to join you. Interact with Him, just like you would a friend. Share how your day has been or ask Him how He's doing. You'll be surprised the things He'll share with you.

Reflection
What did Jesus share with you in this encounter?

_____

_____

_____

_____

_____

How impactful do you feel this encounter was on your over all day?

_____

_____

_____

_____

_____

What are some other ideas for getting a few moments with Jesus throughout your day?

_____

_____

_____

_____

_____

Takeaways From This Encounter With Jesus

ENCOUNTER JESUS:
DAY 8

Activation
Exercise with Jesus.

Instructions
Invite Jesus into your workout time and allow Him to speak to you about how to best take care of *your* body. If you don't or can't workout, use this time to ask Jesus the same question.

Reflection
What strategies did Jesus reveal to you for taking care of your body?

_____

_____

_____

_____

_____

How did it feel inviting Jesus into this area of your life?

_____

_____

_____

_____

_____

What is one thing you want to do to take care of your body in light of this encounter with Jesus?

_____

_____

_____

_____

_____

Takeaways From This Encounter With Jesus

ENCOUNTER JESUS:
DAY 9

Activation
Eat dinner with Jesus.

Instructions
Bring a journal and as you sit and eat dinner with Jesus take time to write down what He shares with you.

Reflection
What did Jesus reveal to you during this encounter?

_____

_____

_____

_____

_____

What was your favorite part of this encounter with Jesus?

_____

_____

_____

_____

_____

What testimony could you share with others from this encounter with Jesus?

_____

_____

_____

_____

_____

Takeaways From This Encounter With Jesus

_____

_____

_____

_____

_____

_____

_____

_____

_____

_____

_____

_____

_____

_____

_____

_____

_____

_____

_____

_____

_____

_____

_____

_____

_____

_____

_____

_____

_____

_____

_____

ENCOUNTER JESUS:
DAY 10

Activation
Fall asleep with Jesus.

Instructions
Before you fall asleep spend time reflecting your day with Jesus. Ask Him to share His favorite part of spending the day with you.

Reflection
What did Jesus share about the day that stuck out to you?

_____

_____

_____

_____

_____

How did reflecting on the day with Jesus impact you?

_____

_____

_____

_____

_____

Moving forward, how do you want to continue to invite Jesus into your daily routine?

_____

_____

_____

_____

_____

Takeaways From This Encounter With Jesus

CHAPTER 15

HANGING OUT WITH JESUS

Congratulations on completing the first ten days of this journey. Today begins another practical series of encounters – doing things with Jesus. Jesus is all about relationship. He died to restore the connection that was lost. Biblically, we see Jesus spending time with people doing things like fishing and eating. He even went to a party and turned water into wine.

He wants to spend time with you doing things you enjoy, like you would spend time with a friend. I pray that you would encounter Jesus and grow in your awareness of Him and intimacy with Him. I declare that your relationship with Him would continue to be strengthened in love, joy, peace, and hope. May you be confident in His delight and love for you as they increase more and more!

ENCOUNTER JESUS:
DAY 11

Activation

Have coffee with Jesus.

Instructions

Jesus wants to have coffee with you. Make your favorite cup of coffee or tea and find a comfortable spot where you can sit with Jesus and avoid distractions. Grab a journal to write down what Jesus shares with you.

Reflection

Describe this encounter with Jesus.

_____

_____

_____

_____

_____

What did Jesus show you that stuck out the most in this encounter?

_____

_____

_____

_____

What is one thing you learned about Jesus today?

_____

_____

_____

_____

_____

Takeaways From This Encounter With Jesus

ENCOUNTER JESUS:
DAY 12

Activation
Create with Jesus.

Instructions
Jesus wants to spend time with you being creative. Grab a pencil, pen or even crayons, markers, or paint and create a piece of art with Jesus.

Reflection
What did you learn about creativity through this encounter with Jesus?

_____

_____

_____

_____

_____

How could you bless someone creatively in partnership with Jesus?

_____

_____

_____

_____

_____

What have you discovered about Jesus today?

_____

_____

_____

_____

_____

Takeaways From This Encounter With Jesus

ENCOUNTER JESUS:
DAY 13

Activation
Make a vision board with Jesus.

Instructions
Grab any material you think you will need. Spend time asking Jesus for specific blueprints and vision for your life and make a vision board reflecting what He shares with you.

Reflection
How would you describe His vision for your life?

_____

_____

_____

_____

_____

How did Jesus' perspective of your future compare with your own perspective?

_____

_____

_____

_____

_____

What did you enjoy most about this encounter?

_____

_____

_____

_____

_____

Takeaways From This Encounter With Jesus

ENCOUNTER JESUS:
DAY 14

Activation
Soak in the presence of Jesus.

Instructions
Go to YouTube, search for "Dappy T Keys", and choose whatever music title that Jesus highlights to you. Get comfortable and focus on Him as the music plays. Allow Jesus to speak to you.

Reflection
What did you experience through your five senses during this encounter with Jesus?

_____

_____

_____

_____

_____

Was it easy or difficult to connect with His presence? Why?

_____

_____

_____

_____

_____

What revelation can you take away from this encounter with Jesus?

_____

_____

_____

_____

_____

Takeaways From This Encounter With Jesus

ENCOUNTER JESUS:
DAY 15

Activation
Journal with Jesus.

Instructions
Jesus wants to speak to you. Grab a journal and find a comfortable spot. Write down a question you have for Jesus. Take time to listen to and write down His answer. Repeat as long as you like.

Reflection
What did Jesus share that touched you the most? Why?

_____

_____

_____

_____

_____

How do you prefer to communicate with Jesus? (reading, writing, etc.) Why?

_____

_____

_____

_____

What is one revelation you are taking away from this encounter?

_____

_____

_____

_____

Takeaways From This Encounter With Jesus

ENCOUNTER JESUS:
DAY 16

Activation
Watch a movie with Jesus.

Instructions
Go to your favorite source for movies (DVD, Redbox, Netflix, etc.) and ask Jesus to highlight a movie for you to watch together. Invite Jesus to speak to you through the movie.

Reflection
How did you see the Kingdom in this movie?

_____

_____

_____

_____

_____

What revelation did Jesus share with you through this movie?

_____

_____

_____

_____

What is another movie you would like to watch with Jesus?

_____

_____

_____

_____

Takeaways From This Encounter With Jesus

_____

_____

_____

_____

_____

_____

_____

_____

_____

_____

_____

_____

_____

_____

_____

_____

_____

_____

_____

_____

_____

_____

_____

_____

_____

_____

_____

_____

_____

ENCOUNTER JESUS:
DAY 17

Activation
Take a personality test with Jesus.

Instructions
Go to www.personalityhacker.com and take the free personality test. Read through your results with Jesus. Ask Him to share His thoughts.

Reflection
What did you learn about your personality?

_____

_____

_____

_____

_____

How does this information impact your identity?

_____

_____

_____

_____

_____

What was the most encouraging part of this encounter with Jesus?

_____

_____

_____

_____

_____

Takeaways From This Encounter With Jesus

ENCOUNTER JESUS:
DAY 18

Activation
Take communion with Jesus.

Instructions
Jesus wants to celebrate communion with you. Find a place where you can be alone with Jesus. Ask Jesus to speak to you as you share communion together.

Reflection
What did Jesus reveal to you about His nature through this encounter?

_____

_____

_____

_____

_____

How do you think the act of taking communion in the natural impacts the spiritual realm?

_____

_____

_____

_____

_____

How you have seen the power of Jesus' blood working recently?

_____

_____

_____

_____

Takeaways From This Encounter With Jesus

ENCOUNTER JESUS:
DAY 19

Activation
Bake something with Jesus.

Instructions
Choose something to bake and invite Jesus to spend time with you. Talk to Jesus as you bake together.

Reflection
How did you experience Jesus during this encounter?

_____

_____

_____

_____

_____

What revelation did Jesus share with you through this encounter?

_____

_____

_____

_____

_____

How can you apply this revelation to your every day life?

_____

_____

_____

_____

_____

Takeaways From This Encounter With Jesus

_____

_____

_____

_____

_____

_____

_____

_____

_____

_____

_____

_____

_____

_____

_____

_____

_____

_____

_____

_____

_____

_____

_____

_____

_____

_____

_____

_____

_____

_____

ENCOUNTER JESUS:
DAY 20

Activation
Choose an activity you enjoy to do with Jesus.

Instructions
Make a plan for spending this time with Jesus. Spend time sharing your heart with Jesus as you enjoy this time together.

Reflection
Why did you choose this specific activity with Jesus?

_____

_____

_____

_____

_____

How did Jesus respond to what you shared with Him?

_____

_____

_____

_____

_____

What is one way you can be intentional about sharing your heart with Jesus?

_____

_____

_____

_____

_____

Takeaways From This Encounter With Jesus

CHAPTER 16

GOING PLACES WITH JESUS

Looking at the life of Jesus, He went places with His friends. We see Him in the garden praying with His three closest friends, in the Upper Room sharing a meal with the twelve disciples, and calling Zacchaeus down from the tree so He could go over to his house. Jesus is relational through and through. He loves spending time with you!

This book is a product of going places with Jesus. A few years ago I scheduled a week long trip with Jesus to Bethel Church in Redding, California. I was looking forward to attending some services, but most excited about spending time with Jesus at the prayer house and in the beautiful garden surrounding it. Two weeks before our trip I woke up one morning and before I could get out of bed He started speaking to me. He asked me to write this book during our trip and gave me specific instructions to write it in the Hebrews coffee shop inside the church. One the last day of my trip I sat in Hebrews finishing up the last of the encounter activations when a woman approached me and asked what brought me to Redding. I introduced myself and told her I was writing a book (never thought those words would ever come out of my mouth!). The barista called her name and after she grabbed her coffee she came back over and handed me her business card. She just happened to be the lead editor of a well-known Christian publishing company! Jesus set me up for a divine appointment that I never could have created myself. Moments like these are why I love doing life with Jesus!

The last ten days of your journey you will spend time going out and spending time with Jesus. Some of the activities may or may not be things that you would normally do or place you would normally go. I encourage you to keep an open mind and trust the process of encountering Jesus. Sometimes we have to get outside of our comfort zones to encounter Him in new and deeper ways. Also, feel free to take more than ten consecutive days to complete this section as it may take some planning.

I declare that Jesus will encounter you in ways that are beyond anything you've ever asked or imagined!

ENCOUNTER JESUS:
DAY 21

Activation
Go to the park with Jesus.

Instructions
Take something to write with and something to write on and go to your favorite park and pick a spot to hang out with Jesus.

Reflection
Describe this encounter with Jesus.

_____

_____

_____

_____

_____

What have you discovered about Jesus today?

_____

_____

_____

_____

What have you discovered about yourself today?

_____

_____

_____

_____

Takeaways From This Encounter With Jesus

_____

_____

_____

_____

_____

_____

_____

_____

_____

_____

_____

_____

_____

_____

_____

_____

_____

_____

_____

_____

_____

_____

_____

_____

_____

_____

_____

_____

_____

_____

ENCOUNTER JESUS:
DAY 22

Activation
Go out to coffee with Jesus.

Instructions
Take something to write with and something to write on and go to a coffee shop you've never tried before. Once you've ordered your favorite drink and/or treat sit down and talk to Jesus. Write down what He shares with you.

Reflection
In what ways were you encouraged to think differently through this encounter with Jesus?

_____

_____

_____

_____

_____

What impacted you the most from this encounter with Jesus?

_____

_____

_____

_____

_____

What is a one thing you are taking away from this experience?

_____

_____

_____

_____

_____

Takeaways From This Encounter With Jesus

ENCOUNTER JESUS:
DAY 23

Activation
Go on a picnic with Jesus.

Instructions
Pack your lunch. Take Jesus to a spot you enjoy outdoors. Spend time listening to Jesus share His heart with you.

Reflection
What did Jesus share with you?

_____

_____

_____

_____

_____

What is something you learned about Jesus' heart today?

_____

_____

_____

_____

_____

Moving forward, how do you want to engage with Jesus in light of this encounter?

_____

_____

_____

_____

_____

Takeaways From This Encounter With Jesus

_____

_____

_____

_____

_____

_____

_____

_____

_____

_____

_____

_____

_____

_____

_____

_____

_____

_____

_____

_____

_____

_____

_____

_____

_____

_____

_____

_____

ENCOUNTER JESUS:
DAY 24

Activation
Go on a photo shoot with Jesus.

Instructions
Grab your phone, iPad, or camera and go to a favorite outdoor location. Take pictures of the surroundings with Jesus.

Reflection
What did Jesus reveal to you through your camera lens?

_____

_____

_____

_____

_____

What scriptures remind you of this encounter with Jesus?

_____

_____

_____

_____

_____

How did you experience glory through this encounter with Jesus?

_____

_____

_____

_____

_____

Takeaways From This Encounter With Jesus

ENCOUNTER JESUS:
DAY 25

Activation
Go for a walk with Jesus.

Instructions
Invite Jesus to take a walk with you. Ask Him to speak to you about direction. Take time to record what He shares with you.

Reflection
What is your favorite part about spending this time with Jesus?

_____

_____

_____

_____

_____

What did Jesus reveal to you today?

_____

_____

_____

_____

_____

What is the next step in obeying what Jesus shared with you today?

_____

_____

_____

_____

_____

Takeaways From This Encounter With Jesus

_____

_____

_____

_____

_____

_____

_____

_____

_____

_____

_____

_____

_____

_____

_____

_____

_____

_____

_____

_____

_____

_____

_____

_____

_____

_____

_____

_____

_____

ENCOUNTER JESUS:
DAY 26

Activation
Go stargazing with Jesus.

Instructions
Find a comfortable spot to sit and enjoy the stars with Him. Listen as He speaks to you about your future.

Reflection
What did Jesus reveal to you tonight?

_____

_____

_____

_____

_____

How did Jesus' perspective of your future compare with your own perspective?

_____

_____

_____

_____

_____

What did you enjoy most about this encounter?

_____

_____

_____

_____

_____

Takeaways From This Encounter With Jesus

_____

_____

_____

_____

_____

_____

_____

_____

_____

_____

_____

_____

_____

_____

_____

_____

_____

_____

_____

_____

_____

_____

_____

_____

_____

_____

_____

_____

_____

_____

ENCOUNTER JESUS:
DAY 27

Activation
Go get dessert with Jesus.

Instructions
Choose where you'd like to get dessert. Once you get your dessert, find a place where you can enjoy your dessert and talk with Jesus.

Reflection
What did you learn about your relationship with Jesus?

_____

_____

_____

_____

_____

How impactful do you feel this encounter was for you?

_____

_____

_____

_____

_____

What are other fun ways you can spend time with Jesus in the future?

_____

_____

_____

_____

_____

Takeaways From This Encounter With Jesus

_____

_____

_____

_____

_____

_____

_____

_____

_____

_____

_____

_____

_____

_____

_____

_____

_____

_____

_____

_____

_____

_____

_____

_____

_____

_____

_____

_____

_____

ENCOUNTER JESUS:
DAY 28

Activation
Go to the mall with Jesus.

Instructions
Pick a location in the mall to people-watch with Jesus. Allow Him to show you how He sees others.

Reflection
What stuck out to you the most during this encounter with Jesus?

_____

_____

_____

_____

_____

Describe your people-watching experience. Was it fun, awkward, enlightening, etc.?

_____

_____

_____

_____

_____

What is one way you can actively love others like Jesus on a daily basis?

_____

_____

_____

_____

_____

Takeaways From This Encounter With Jesus

ENCOUNTER JESUS:
DAY 29

Activation
Go spend time with Jesus in nature.

Instructions
Pick your favorite local spot in nature and invite Jesus to come along. Spend time talking with Jesus and admiring creation.

Reflection
What did Jesus reveal to you during this encounter?

_____

_____

_____

_____

_____

What did Jesus share that impacted you the most?

_____

_____

_____

_____

_____

What are you taking away from this time with Jesus?

_____

_____

_____

_____

_____

Takeaways From This Encounter With Jesus

_____

_____

_____

_____

_____

_____

_____

_____

_____

_____

_____

_____

_____

_____

_____

_____

_____

_____

_____

_____

_____

_____

_____

_____

_____

_____

_____

_____

_____

_____

_____

ENCOUNTER JESUS:
DAY 30

Activation
Create your own encounter with Jesus.

Instructions
Do something with Jesus that you enjoy. Engage with Him in relationship...
share, listen, create, ask questions, etc. Enjoy the freedom you have to build
your own relationship with Him.

Reflection
What did you think/feel about the experience of creating your own encounter
with Jesus?

_____

_____

_____

_____

_____

What did you enjoy most about this encounter with Jesus?

_____

_____

_____

_____

What is one thing you learned about Jesus today?

_____

_____

_____

_____

Takeaways From This Encounter With Jesus

WHAT NOW?

Congratulations on completing this thirty-day journey of encountering with Jesus! Take time to reflect on your journey...

Reflection

Which encounter with Jesus was the most impactful for you?

_____

_____

_____

_____

_____

What was your favorite encounter with Jesus?

_____

_____

_____

_____

_____

How have you grown in your *awareness* of Jesus through this experience?

_____

_____

_____

_____

_____

How have you grown in your *intimacy* with Jesus through this experience?

_____

_____

_____

_____

_____

It's your job to take it from here. Do what works best for *your* relationship with Jesus. Have fun. Go deep. Share needs. Express wants. Dream together. Explore. Be creative. You've got this!

Here are a few more tips for creating your own encounters with Jesus…

- Ask Jesus what He'd like to do when you spend time with Him
- Do something you've never done before
- Try things outside of your comfort zone
- Regularly ask Jesus to show you how scripture pertains to situations, circumstances, and environments
- When you want to know more or don't understand something ask Jesus questions

Finally, I want to leave you with Paul's prayer for the *Ephesians 3:17-19*, "And I pray that you, being rooted and established in love, may have power, together with all the saints, to grasp how wide and long and high and deep is the love of Christ, and to know this love that surpasses knowledge – that you may be filled to the measure of all the fullness of God".

ABOUT THE AUTHOR

Sarah Crockett is a coach, teacher, leader, speaker, and atmosphere shifter. She enjoys creating life-changing encounters with God's presence that bring revelation, healing, and deliverance. Sarah has spent over a decade influencing college students for the Kingdom in both university and ministry settings. She initiated the concept of "Go Week" at Florida State University where multiple ministries unite to spend a week each fall semester serving incoming students. Sarah has also spent over a decade in college ministry activating students to know and release God's presence. She enjoys "finding the gold" in others while equipping them to know and release God's presence. She has travelled for ministry both nationally and internationally. Most notably to Russia, Finland, Haiti, and several cities throughout Mexico.

beENCOUNTERed is an expression of her passion to know and release God's presence. Sarah had a personal encounter with Jesus, at age 14, while watching the sun rise over the mountains of North Carolina. At age 16, she had an encounter where she was enveloped by God's wrap-around presence. These two encounters transformed her life. She enjoys creatively activating others to have their own personal encounters and has been inspired by a quote from Kevin Dedmon, "God wants us to have an encounter, so that we become an encounter, so that others can have an encounter". She believes one moment in the presence of God can change everything!

Sarah also enjoys quality time with family and friends, laughing, a good cup of dark roast coffee, spending time in the mountains, traveling, and spending time with her furry friend Hammy P. Cat!

ADDITIONAL RESOURCES

ENCOUNTER ACTIVATION SERIES

Five Practical Keys For Having Encounters With God

A Simple Tool For Hearing The Voice Of God

15 Questions For Strengthening Your Connection With The Heart Of God

TOOLS FOR COMING UP HIGHER

Discovering Your Lens For Life

Becoming More You Self Assessment

www.beENCOUNTERed.com

CONNECT WITH SARAH

Web

www.beENCOUNTERed.com

Facebook

https://www.facebook.com/beencountered

Instagram

https://www.instagram.com/beencountered

85604654R00073

Made in the USA
Middletown, DE
25 August 2018